A Catalog for the Qualitative Interpretation of the House-Tree-Person (H-T-P)

Isaac Jolles
School Psychologist

Published by

WESTERN PSYCHOLOGICAL SERVICES
Publishers and Distributors
12031 Wilshire Boulevard
Los Angeles, California 90025

Library of Congress Catalog Card Number: 79-57297

International Standard Book Number: 0-87424-001-8

EIGHTH PRINTING .... OCTOBER 1983

TABLE OF CONTENTS

FOREWORD

No catalog can be expected to be all-inclusive insofar as points of qualitative analysis of the H-T-P are concerned, nor fully and finally definitive in its interpretations of the points it contains. In all probability, other qualitative aspects will be identified in time, and certain interpretations now made will be amended, amplified, or even discarded. However, during the last 12 years this excellent compendium has been of great help to the H-T-P novice in his or her efforts to become more conversant with the intricacies of qualitative analysis, and it has served more experienced clinicians well as a reference text.

The terms *pathoformic, pathological,* and *pathognomonic* are used in this catalog to indicate the grossly estimated levels of maladjustment suggested by certain interpretations. However, the final interpretation of qualitative points and the assessment of the values to be assigned to them must depend on their relationships to each other and to the total context in which they appear.

A pathoformic sign should make the examiner suspect that the subject exhibiting it would tend to behave deviantly within the area represented directly or symbolically by that sign to a degree that might interfere with the subject's ability to adjust easily and satisfactorily. A pathoformic sign is to be regarded as indicating a possible "danger spot" within the personality; the danger may be potential or actual.

A pathological sign suggests that the deviancy of behavior is considerably greater than pathoformic and is much more likely to be immediate and serious.

A pathognomonic sign implies that a very serious personality maladjustment is present and active. (Note that there are very few single signs in the H-T-P that carry this much weight.)

To conclude, the H-T-P practitioner of any degree of skill and experience will be well advised to use this catalog with the great caution that sound clinical practice demands and the catalog's author so wisely counsels.

John N. Buck
June 1964

ACKNOWLEDGMENTS

The author is indebted greatly to John N. Buck, Selma Landisberg, and Hannah Davis for their contributions to the original catalog. Without their assistance in reviewing the initial manuscript, the catalog would have presented only the materials which were then current to clinicians in the first H-T-P Manual and the Richmond Proceedings, some now modified and some incomplete.

The author is also indebted to Emanuel Hammer for his subsequent publications concerning the H-T-P. His materials have been used extensively in this and the previous revisions of the catalog to supplement the information obtained by the writer in his many clinical studies with this technique over a period of 20 years and his several research studies with children of school age. Finally, John Buck has contributed additional important materials through his recent revised H-T-P Manual as well as correspondence with the writer since the original catalog was published.

Isaac Jolles
1971

HOW TO USE THE H-T-P CATALOG

Early in the author's experience with the H-T-P technique, he observed that much time was spent searching the H-T-P Manual for probable meanings of aspects of a drawing. Although the H-T-P Manual is well organized in explaining the qualitative approach to the interpretation of the drawings, it is less well organized in assisting the examiner with specific interpretive problems. For example, there are a number of variations in branch structure of the Tree, but the significance of these variations is not explained in any one place. It is doubtful that one could write a teaching manual and so organize it that all variations would be in one place, namely, under the topic of "branch structure." Thus, the idea for this catalog was conceived.

The catalog interpretations are presented in a somewhat dogmatic manner. Actually, many of these interpretations are still hypothetical, and *must be interpreted in the context of all factors in the H-T-P, together with the case history and the complete clinical background.* Users of the catalog are advised to keep this caution in mind when they seek meaning and insight in the H-T-P. After all, it is the clinician who makes the diagnosis; the test or technique merely gives clues.

Buck has emphasized the need to avoid attaching significance to an item unless the subject has indicated that the item has significance to him or her through line quality, shading, proportion, comments, and so on. He also cautions the clinician to avoid adhering strictly to general meanings of items because given items may not have such meanings to certain subjects but rather have specific or idiosyncratic meanings. Finally, Buck stresses that an item may arouse positive as well as negative feelings; once the subject has demonstrated that an item has significance for him or her, the clinician must determine if this significance is positive or negative.

It is emphasized that this catalog is not a substitute for a thorough knowledge of the H-T-P literature or adequate professional training in personality dynamics and projective techniques. One not well acquainted with the general, fundamental concepts of the qualitative interpretation of the H-T-P will have difficulty using this catalog. A general knowledge of the H-T-P technique is essential to understand the "definitions" presented and to know where to look for specific items in the catalog.

Furthermore, the H-T-P, like other projective techniques, is not a substitute for sound clinical training. A well-trained clinician will find the H-T-P technique—and this catalog— valuable, but one with meager clinical background will extract little from the H-T-P or this catalog.

This catalog is not an attempt to organize in one place materials from all publications and authorities on the H-T-P. It includes information from the H-T-P Manual (Buck, 1970), the proceedings of the H-T-P workshop at the Veterans Administration Hospital at Richmond, Virginia (Buck, 1950), Hammer's *Clinical Application of Projective Drawings* (1958), Jolles' research with children and color, correspondence with Buck, and empirical findings from Jolles' clinical studies of children. The result brings up to date many interpretive points which have been modified since the publication of the original H-T-P Manual (Buck, 1948).

Some materials are not included in the catalog because they did not lend themselves readily to a catalog type of manual. Also, a few basic concepts are not included because it was felt that readers would be familiar with them if they were well acquainted with the H-T-P Manual.

Examiners should read the full catalog before attempting to use it. This provides orientation and saves time in locating items. In general, examiners will find what they seek, if it is in the catalog, in three places: (1) *General Interpretations* applicable to the three wholes (the first section of Chapter 1, p. 1); (2) sections in Chapter 1 for House (p. 29), Tree (p. 67), and Person (p. 95); and (3) *Post-Drawing Interrogation* (PDI) (Chapter 2).

It is advisable to look under both specific wholes and the General Interpretations section to obtain greater elaboration of meanings. For example, since the groundline means the same in the three drawings, it is in the General Interpretations section rather than in the section on the House. However, occasionally an item is in the General Interpretations section and also in the section on a whole. This is true for the groundline since it is also in the section on the Tree.

The PDI is actually a projective interview and should be interpreted as such. All the examples given in Chapter 2 are taken from actual cases examined by the author, and the interpretations given have been verified by case history material and follow-up interviews with parents and teachers. Thus, clinicians using the PDI should amplify the specific meanings of their patients' responses in this manner. The clinician should use this chapter of the catalog with caution when dealing with an adult subject since only the author's revision of the PDI for children (Jolles, 1956) has been used.

A change from the earlier editions of the catalog is that all interpretations pertaining to color have been grouped together in Chapter 3. Any meanings the clinician may seek pertaining to color may be found under one of four general headings in this chapter: General Interpretations applicable to the three wholes, House, Tree, and Person. All interpretations in this chapter pertain to either the general meaning of given colors or their significance in specific situations. Since most of these interpretations are based on the author's clinical experiences and limited research, all dealing with children and adolescents, the clinician should bear this in mind when using this catalog with an adult.

NOTES

CHAPTER 1
THE ACHROMATIC PHASE
(The Pencil Drawings)

General Interpretations

CLOUDS
- Generalized anxiety referred to situations represented by drawn whole.

DETAILS
- Indicate awareness of, interest in, and ability to deal with and conform to practical or concrete aspects of life. Examiner should note the extent of interest and realism in the details and the relative weight assigned to them, as well as the manner in which the details are organized into a totality.

Easily and noncompulsively drawn
- Good capacity for well-balanced interaction with environment.

Essential, absence of
- Absence of essential details in drawings of subjects known to be or to have recently been of average or higher intelligence frequently is indicative of the onset of intellectual deterioration or severe emotional disturbance. At best it indicates a lack of adequate interest in environment.

Essential, excessive duplication of
- Probably unable to make tactful or flexible relationships with people.

1

NOTES

DETAILS (continued)

Excessive

- "Quantity necessity" indicates compulsive need to structure situation; overconcern with total environment. Type of details employed (relevant, irrelevant, bizarre) may aid in establishing greater specificity or sensitivity.

Intellectual aspects of

- Recognition of and orientation to elementary, concrete aspects of everyday life.

Meticulously drawn

- Obsessive-compulsive tendencies.

Obsessive (specific or implied)

- Unhappily sensitive.

Organization of

- If organizational difficulty shown in three wholes, major emotional disturbance or some organic disturbance, or both, can be suspected.

- If organizational difficulty occurs for one whole, disturbance may be functional rather than organic and related to situations represented by affected whole. Exception may be found in bright subjects with diffuse brain damage. If organization for three wholes is good, basic structure of personality is sound despite many pathoformic signs.

- If organization is better in chromatic than achromatic drawings, prognosis probably is better than if the reverse were true. In children this is true because of the suggestion that the child can respond to warmth (modification of environment more often used in therapy with children than adults).

NOTES

ERASURE
With redrawing
- If redrawing results in improvement, it is a favorable sign. Erasure with subsequent deterioration implies strong emotional reaction to the object being drawn or its symbolization.

Without attempt at redrawing
- Detail arouses strong conflict over detail itself or what detail symbolizes.

FATIGUE, MARKED
- Presence of a depression of mood which may or may not be accompanied by some factor producing diminution of efficiency.

GROUNDLINE
- Insecurity.
- Provides point of reference to construct whole.
- Provides stability for drawn whole.
- Significance sometimes depends upon quality ascribed to groundline by the subject (e.g., "The boy is skating on thin ice"). Least frequently drawn under Person, most frequently under Tree. Induced groundlines are less significant than if spontaneously produced.

Sloping downward and away from drawn whole on either side
- Feeling of isolation and exposure.
- Maternal dependence.
- Need for exhibitionism, depending on size and type of whole as well as the subject's comments.

NOTES

GROUNDLINE (continued)
Sloping downward to right
- Feeling that the future is uncertain and perhaps perilous; degree of feeling seems indicated by degree of precipitancy of line.

Very heavy
- Feelings of anxiety aroused by relationships at reality level.

IDENTIFICATION WITH SELF
- Degree of subjectivity determines interpretation; may range from evidence of mild narrowing of psychological horizon to obvious and convincing evidence of extreme ideas of self-reference because of excessive self-concern or high degree of egocentricity.

LINES
Curving
- Usually healthy sign although may indicate distaste for convention and/or restriction if carried to extreme.

Faintly drawn for specific detail
- Reluctance to express detail in question because of its real or symbolic representation.

Faintly drawn throughout
- Generalized feeling of inadequacy accompanied by insecurity, indecision and/or fear of defeat. If lines become fainter from House through Person, generalized anxiety and/or depression is indicated.

Heavy for specific detail
- Fixation upon object drawn.

NOTES

LINES (continued)

- Hostility, suppressed or overt, against item drawn or what it symbolizes; accompanying anxiety likely.

Heavy on periphery only

- Striving to maintain personality balance; may be unpleasantly aware of this striving and/or experiencing marked body tensions.

Heavy throughout one whole

- Generalized tension associated with aspect of the subject's life represented by the drawn whole.

Heavy throughout three wholes

- Organicity suspected.

- Generalized tension.

Interrupted and never joined

- Feeling of incipient ego collapse.

Rigidly straight

- Internal rigidity.

Scribbled

- Characterized by uninterrupted and partially overlapping ovals; resembles child's scribbling. Most frequently observed in peripheral outline of Tree's branch structure, hair of Person, and smoke from chimney of House.

- Important indicator of organicity.

Sketchy, persistent use of

- At best, need exists for exactitude and meticulosity.

- At worst, pathoformic sign suggesting inability to be definite.

NOTES

MOUNTAINS IN BACKGROUND
- Defensive attitude and need for dependence, often maternal dependence.

PAPER-BASING
- Generalized insecurity.

- Depression of mood tone; the smaller the drawing and/or fainter the lines, the more marked the depression.

PAPER-CHOPPING
Base of page
- Is detectable only by questioning the subject concerning paper-based whole, or by the subject's spontaneous comments.

- The further the drawn whole extends below the page's base, the greater the likelihood that suppression has been employed pathoformically to maintain personality integrity. Suggests strong potential for explosive action.

Left side of whole
- Fixation on past with fear of future.
- Overconcern with frank, uninhibited, emotional experiences.
- Tendency toward compulsive behavior.

Right side of whole
- Desire to escape into future to get away from past.
- Fear of frank, uninhibited, emotional experience.
- Tendency to exercise strong control.

Top of page
- Fixation upon fantasy to seek satisfaction not obtainable from reality.

NOTES

PAPER-SIDING

- Implies space constriction with resultant height-ened sensitivity and strong suggestion of aggressive-reactive tendencies, suppressed or not.

PAPER-TOPPING

- Tendency toward fixation on thinking and fantasy as sources of satisfaction. Satisfaction may or may not be obtainable by this mechanism.

PAPER-TURNING

- Aggressive and/or negativistic tendencies.
- Pathoformic if occurring more than once.
- Perseveration indicated if paper-turning always in same direction.

PERSPECTIVE

- Through use of perspective, the subject may reveal attitudes and feelings toward and understanding of broader and more complex relationships to be made with environment and people, and methods of coping with such relationships.

Intellectual aspects of

- Ability to evaluate environment, personal relationships, and people on broader and more specific basis.

Profiles facing opposite customary direction

- Represents recognition of hostile impulses the subject consciously tries to suppress and/or sublimate.

Wholes drawn entirely without profile suggestion

- When three wholes are drawn full-face, the subject is essentially rigid and uncompromising. Such determination to face everything directly may be reaction formation to basic underlying insecurities.

NOTES

PERSPECTIVE (continued)
Wholes drawn far away
- Desire to withdraw from conventional society and/or feeling of isolation or rejection.

Wholes drawn in absolute profile
(Pertains to House with side towards viewer and no visible door on that side; Person with one side, only one arm and one leg, visible to viewer)

- Reluctance to face environment directly.

- Definite desire to withdraw.

- Hiding one's inner self.

- Making contact with people or reality only on one's terms.

- Paranoid attitudes.

PLACEMENT OF WHOLE
Above average midpoint of form page
- The higher the midpoint of whole above the average midpoint, the greater is the implication that the subject: (1) feels he or she is striving strongly and goal is relatively unattainable; (2) seeks satisfaction in fantasy (intratensivity); (3) keeps self aloof, relatively inaccessible. Average midpoint varies with age (see Table 1).

Below average midpoint of form page
- The farther the midpoint of whole below the average midpoint, the greater the likelihood that the subject: (1) feels insecure and inadequate and feeling moves toward depression of mood; (2) is reality bound (concrete, extratensive). Average midpoint varies with age (see Table 1).

In absolute center of form page
- Insecurity and rigidity.

NOTES

PLACEMENT OF WHOLE (continued)
- Need to maintain psychological equilibrium by careful control.

In upper left-hand corner of form page
- Markedly anxious or regressed.

- Tendency to shun new experiences.

- Desire to return to past and/or remain absorbed in fantasy.

Table 1

**Means and Sigmas for Vertical Placement of Each Whole
By Sex and Age**

Drawing	Sex	Age								Mean
		5	6	7	8	9	10	11	12	
House	Male	.11 (.93)	.03 (.93)	.01 (.80)	−.04 (.77)	.09 (.95)	.12 (.84)	.24 (.64)	.29 (.59)	.11 (.82)
	Female	.07 (.98)	.02 (.75)	−.17 (.76)	−.03 (.46)	.16 (.54)	.20 (.63)	.33 (.64)	.50 (.64)	.14 (.71)
	Total	.09 (.95)	.03 (.85)	−.08 (.79)	−.04 (.62)	.13 (.77)	.16 (.74)	.29 (.64)	.40 (.63)	.13 (.77)
Tree	Male	−.24 (.86)	−.19 (.81)	−.37 (.75)	−.20 (.65)	.00 (.80)	−.04 (.57)	.10 (.55)	.23 (.41)	−.08 (.71)
	Female	−.06 (.92)	−.44 (.91)	−.35 (.67)	−.16 (.41)	.07 (.41)	.06 (.48)	.17 (.47)	.25 (.57)	−.05 (.67)
	Total	−.15 (.89)	−.31 (.87)	−.36 (.71)	−.18 (.54)	.02 (.63)	.02 (.53)	.14 (.51)	.24 (.50)	−.07 (.69)
Person	Male	−.11 (.90)	−.37 (1.15)	−.79 (1.33)	−.44 (.99)	−.33 (1.07)	−.23 (.97)	−.03 (.90)	.09 (.61)	−.27 (1.05)
	Female	−.01 (1.03)	−.63 (1.45)	−.49 (.98)	−.47 (.76)	−.13 (.85)	−.01 (.78)	.10 (.77)	.27 (.85)	−.16 (1.00)
	Total	−.06 (.97)	−.50 (1.31)	−.64 (1.18)	−.45 (.89)	−.21 (1.00)	−.12 (.89)	.04 (.84)	.18 (.75)	−.22 (1.02)

Note. Minus signs (−) indicate placement below geometric center. All numbers in terms of one inch or fraction thereof.

Sigmas are in parentheses.

Reprinted by special permission of *Journal of Clinical Psychology*.

NOTES

PLACEMENT OF WHOLE (continued)
On left side of form page
- Emotional dominance.

- Stressing past.

- Impulsiveness.

- Extratensive.

- Average midpoint varies with age (see Table 2).

On right side of form page
- Tends to seek satisfaction in intellectual areas.

- Intratensive.

- Controlled behavior.

- Stressing future.

- Average midpoint varies with age (see Table 2).

PROPORTION
- Reality and relativity of proportional values expressed in drawings reveal values assigned to things, situations, persons, etc., that drawings or parts of drawings represent actually or symbolically.

Intellectual aspects of
- Judgment, implying type of thinking or planning concerned largely with immediate and concrete aspects of things.

Relationship to minimum of details
- A subject with good proportional and spatial relationships but bare minimum of details appears to have: (1) tendency to withdraw, (2) "abnormal" disregard of conventional matters.

- A subject with inferior understanding of proportional and spatial relationships and minimum of

NOTES

PROPORTION (continued)

details is presumed: (1) mentally deficient, (2) suffering marked diminution of intellectual efficiency which may be irreversible.

PSYCHOMOTOR DECREASE, PERSISTENT

- Suggests presence of organic factor, crippling anxiety, or severe depression.

Table 2

Means and Sigmas for Horizontal Placement of Each Whole By Sex and Age

Drawing	Sex	5	6	7	8	9	10	11	12	Mean
	Male	−.37 (.99)	−.16 (1.06)	−.16 (.99)	−.43 (.98)	−.22 (.84)	−.12 (.72)	.01 (.79)	.03 (.72)	−.16 (.90)
House	Female	−.07 (.86)	−.33 (.92)	−.26 (.98)	−.28 (.90)	.20 (.96)	−.04 (.77)	−.04 (.72)	−.02 (.72)	−.10 (.87)
	Total	−.22 (.94)	−.24 (1.00)	−.21 (.99)	−.35 (.94)	−.01 (.93)	−.08 (.75)	−.01 (.76)	−.01 (.72)	−.13 (.89)
	Male	−.01 (.89)	−.24 (.83)	−.25 (.66)	−.25 (.55)	−.36 (.68)	−.13 (.55)	−.20 (.52)	−.21 (.51)	−.21 (.51)
Tree	Female	−.08 (.72)	−.36 (.73)	−.28 (.62)	−.17 (.64)	−.17 (.62)	−.19 (.43)	−.30 (.55)	−.30 (.43)	−.24 (.59)
	Total	−.05 (.82)	−.29 (.79)	−.26 (.60)	−.21 (.60)	−.27 (.65)	−.16 (.49)	−.25 (.52)	−.26 (.47)	−.22 (.60)
	Male	−.26 (.88)	−.28 (.83)	−.29 (.64)	−.31 (.56)	−.40 (.61)	−.33 (.54)	−.36 (.55)	−.31 (.60)	−.32 (.66)
Person	Female	−.10 (.79)	−.40 (.62)	−.18 (.55)	−.27 (.48)	−.18 (.52)	−.35 (.59)	−.39 (.54)	−.34 (.53)	−.28 (.59)
	Total	−.18 (.84)	−.34 (.74)	−.23 (.60)	−.29 (.52)	−.29 (.57)	−.34 (.56)	−.37 (.55)	−.33 (.56)	−.30 (.62)

Note. Minus signs (−) indicate placement below geometric center. All numbers in terms of one inch or fraction thereof.

Sigmas are in parentheses.

Reprinted by special permission of *Journal of Clinical Psychology*.

NOTES

PSYCHOMOTOR INCREASE, MARKED
- Excessive stimulability with concomitant but limited inhibitory power.

REDRAWING WITHOUT ERASURE OF ORIGINAL
- Negativistic reaction.

REINFORCEMENT
General
- Free-floating anxiety; fear of losing control.

Specific
- Fixation upon object drawn or represented symbolically; fixation on action or attitude, often with anxiety.

SEQUENCE: SEGMENT BY SEGMENT
- Insecurity due to inability to visualize whole as unitary concept and feeling of imbalance.
- Common in organics or severe anxiety states.

SHADING
Pathoformic use of
- Anxiety.

Unemphasized use of
- Sensitive, not necessarily unhappily sensitive, to relationships with others.

SHADOW
- Conflict situation producing anxiety at conscious level when shadow produced spontaneously and before sun is induced.
- Compulsivity if shadow added after sun has been induced.

See *Tree: Shadow*, p. 79.

NOTES

SPACE CONSTRICTION

- Feeling of much frustration produced by restricting environment, concomitant with feelings of hostility and desire to react aggressively, which may be carried out.

- Feelings of strong tension and irritability.

- Feelings of helpless immobility; feet or portion of legs of Person or base of Tree chopped off by bottom of page.

SUN

- Symbol of authoritative figure; often seen as source of power and/or warmth; frequently identified as father or mother.

TRANSPARENCY

- Reality denied.

- Indication of the degree that personality is disrupted by the presence of emotional or organic factors, or both, causing interference with reality testing.

- Pathological significance gauged by: (1) number of transparencies; (2) magnitude of transparency; (3) location of transparency (e.g., sleeve of coat less meaningful than wall of House).

WEATHER, KIND OF

- Subject's feeling of environment. The more severe and unpleasant the weather, the greater the likelihood that the subject feels the environment is oppressive and hostile.

- The subject's attitude toward type of weather described must be elicited before interpretation is attempted.

NOTES

WHOLES
Constriction
- Feeling of inadequacy.
- Definite tendency to withdraw.
- Desire to reject whole or what it symbolizes.

Discrepancy in size of chromatic and achromatic
- When the chromatic drawings are much larger than the corresponding achromatic drawings, overreaction to excitement is indicated. Sometimes a subconscious need to be very aggressive may be present. However, it is normal for the chromatic drawings to be a little larger than the achromatic drawings.

- When the achromatic drawings are much larger than the chromatic wholes, there may be a need to avoid pleasurable or excitable stimulation. Sometimes there may be a subconscious desire to withdraw, to be less aggressive.

WIND
- Symbolizes felt pressures over which the subject has little control.

See *Tree: Wind*, p. 91.

NOTES

House

BATHROOM

- Function is elimination and sanitation. Disturbances involving these functions may be indicated when manner of presentation shows significance.

See *Room(s)*, p. 51.

BEDROOM

- Scene of most intimate interpersonal relationships.
- Graphic or verbal treatment of bedroom may provide clues to sexual adjustment.
- Sometimes reveals desire to withdraw.
- May give clues to attitudes of the need for rest and relaxation.

See *Room(s)*, p. 51.

CHIMNEY

- Phallic symbol of significance.
- Sensual maturity and balance.
- Symbol of warmth in intimate relationships.

√Absence of

- Feels home lacks psychological warmth.
- Difficulty dealing with male sex symbol.

Almost completely hidden

- Reluctance to deal with emotion-producing stimuli.
- Castration fear.

Emphasis upon

- Preoccupation with male sex symbol.

NOTES

CHIMNEY (continued)

- May indicate preoccupation with chimney associations.
- Overconcern with warmth.

Multiplicity of

- When significant because of depiction, implies overconcern with phallic symbol and/or intimate relationships.

Overly large

- Overconcern with sexual matters, with the need to demonstrate virility.
- Exhibitionist tendencies.

Penetrated by opening

- Sex role confusion.
- Sexual impotency.
- Castration fear.

Roof angled

- Normal for children under 8 years of age.
- Organicity suspected over 8 years of age.

Transparent or without depth

- Phallic denial which may represent impotence or castration fears.
- Female degradation of male symbol.
- Normal for preadolescent children (without depth).

Visible through transparent wall

- Poorly suppressed exhibitionist tendencies.

NOTES

CHIMNEY (continued)

- Feeling that one's phallic preoccupation is obvious to others.

DETAILS
Degrading

- Usually symbolize feelings of aggressive hostility, at times partially internalized.

- Hostility directed against whole or degraded parts, or symbol of whole or parts.

Essential

- At least one door (unless only side of House is presented), one window, one wall, a roof, and, unless identified as a tropical dwelling, a chimney or egress for smoke from means of heating, or absence of chimney accompanied by damage to House.

Irrelevant

- Need to structure environment more completely, thus connoting feelings of insecurity and inadequacy. The more profuse the irrelevant detailing, the more intense the presumed feeling.

- Overconcern with environment at expense of self.

- In general, the better the irrelevant details are organized and the more intimate their relationship to the House, the greater the likelihood that anxiety is well channelized and controlled.

See specific detail (*Shrubs, Walkway*, etc.).

Irrelevant, horizontal line separating first and second stories

- Suggests extreme concretivity with possible organicity and/or fixation upon the *soma*.

- Presence of psychosomatic disorders suspected.

NOTES

DINING ROOM

- Function pertains to satisfaction of oral and nutritional needs. Disturbances involving these functions indicated if presentation significant.

  See *Room(s)*, p. 51.

DOOR(S)

Above baseline and without steps

- Inaccessibility.

- Tends to contact others on own terms.

Absence of

- Pathoformic difficulty in becoming accessible to others, particularly in home.

Back or side

- Egress, escape, particularly when door is significant.

Front

- Index to accessibility.

- Represents most direct ingress and egress.

Last drawn detail

- Distaste for interpersonal contacts.

- Tendency to withdraw from reality.

Open

- If House occupied, strong need to receive warmth from without or demonstrate accessibility.

- If House unoccupied, feeling of lack of ego defense.

Side

- Egress, escape.

NOTES

DOORS (continued)

- If only door drawn, marked inaccessibility.

Very large

- Overdependence on others and/or need to impress with social accessibility.

Very small

- Reluctance to permit access to self.

- Feelings of inadequacy and indecision relative to social situations.

With formidable lock

- Hostility, suspicious withdrawal, defensiveness.

With heavy hinges

- Hostility, suspicious withdrawal, defensiveness.

DOORKNOB, EMPHASIS UPON

- Overconsciousness of door's function and/or phallic preoccupation.

EAVES, EMPHASIS UPON, BY REINFORCEMENT OR EXTENSION BEYOND WALLS

- Overly defensive attitude; usually suspicious.

ENDWALL

Lines heavy for this detail specifically

- Struggling to maintain contact with reality.

Reversal of presentation according to handedness

Conscious effort to control or conform with concomitant strong feelings of rebellion.

FENCE AROUND HOUSE

- Need for protection from threat of environment.

NOTES

FENCE AROUND HOUSE (continued)

- May also represent a need to keep others from learning about inner feelings and attitudes.

FIREPLACE
Direct emphasis upon
(Fireplace seen through walls of House)

- Fixation upon direct function of fireplace, as warmth giving, or upon symbolism of fireplace, as female or male genitalia, etc.

- Magnitude indicated by denial of reality (non-transparency of wall) which results in depiction of fireplace.

- Interpretation ultimately depends on treatment accorded fireplace and comments about it.

Indirect emphasis upon
(As indicated in PDI)

- Conflict with person customarily occupying room.

- Neurotic attachment to person customarily occupying room or emotion-producing situation associated with that person. Emotion aroused by room's function as bathroom, living room, dining room, etc.

FLOOR PLAN DRAWN INSTEAD OF HOUSE

- Severe conflict in home. If plan well-presented, presence of paranoid ideation suspected; if plan poorly presented, organicity suspected.

FLOWERS, TULIP OR DAISY-LIKE

- Insecurity due to need to structure environment.

- Frequently represents persons identified in PDI.

NOTES

FOUNDATION PILLARS, ABNORMALLY HIGH
- Organicity suspected.
- Precarious reality contact.

FURNACE, INDIRECT EMPHASIS UPON
- Pleasant warmth or frank hostility relative to home.

GUTTERS
- Heightened attitude to defensiveness and usually suspiciousness.

HOUSE
- Present home.
- Home as the subject would like it to be.
- Unsatisfying home of past.
- Satisfying home of past.
- Attitude toward family and/or interpretation of family's feelings toward the subject.
- Self-portrait.
- When married adult regards House as childhood home, likelihood exists of regression or fixation.

Anthropomorphic concept of
- Organicity suspected unless produced by young child.

Distant
- Striving and/or feeling rejected, or rejecting someone.
- Feels inaccessible, or home beyond ability to cope with.
- If drawn concept is reverse of PDI, serious reality-testing flaw may be present.

NOTES

HOUSE (continued)

Filthy, rotten, etc.
- May be expressing feelings about self.
- Hostility towards home.

Nearby
- Attainability and/or feeling of warmth and welcome.

Rear view drawn
- Withdrawal and oppositional tendencies.
- Paranoid attitudes.

KITCHEN
- Where food is prepared; thus, if manner of presentation is significant of disturbance, oral eroticism may be indicated; possibly related to strong need for affection.

See *Room(s)*, p. 51.

LIVING ROOM
- Social intercourse.

See *Room(s)*, p. 51.

MOVEMENT
- Probably pathological, at least pathoformic. Symbolizes feelings of crippling loss of ego control. Occurs far less frequently for House than Tree or Person.

OUTHOUSE
- Aggression against owner of the House; or rebellion against the subject's concepts of artificial cultural standards, especially when drawn beside obviously modern home.

NOTES

OUTHOUSE (continued)

- If outhouse is outdoor toilet, urethral and/or anal preoccupations may be suspected.

PAPER-BASING

- Usually representative of basic insecurity in situations involving home and/or more intimate relationships.

See *General Interpretations: Paper-Basing,* p. 11.

PAPER-SIDING

- Generalized insecurity.

- Frequently indicates insecurity which has: (1) specific temporal meaning (page's left for past, right for future); (2) specific meaning associated with use of room so sided or its customary occupant; (3) specific experiential meaning (page's left for emotional, right for intellectual).

See *General Interpretations: Paper-Chopping,* p. 11.

PAPER-TOPPING

- Seldom in drawings of House.

- Suggests chaotic retreat from reality.

PERSPECTIVE

Above subject (worm's-eye view)

- A feeling either of rejection from home or of striving towards a home or home situation which the subject feels unlikely to attain.

- A desire to withdraw, to make only limited contact with other persons.

Below subject (bird's-eye view)

- Rejection of drawn House.

NOTES

PERSPECTIVE (continued)

- Rejection of common tendency to glorify "home."
- Iconoclastic attitudes.
- Feeling of being above usual emotional and restrictive home ties, often with concomitant depressive feelings.

"Loss of perspective" sign
(Produces a good endwall and roof at one end then finds it impossible to produce adequate representation of depth at opposite end of House and draws vertical endline for roof and wall)

- Fear of future (if vertical endline is to right) or desire to forget past (if vertical endline is to left) may be indicative of organicity.

Triple
(Four or more distinct walls, no two intended to be in same plane)

- Desires to know everything that is taking place around the subject.
- Overconcern with feelings about the subject by those in the subject's environment.
- Attempt to restructure completely all superficial aspects of self.

PROFILE, ABSOLUTE

- Acute paranoid reaction toward home and/or most intimate interpersonal relations is suggested.

RAIN SPOUTS

- Heightened attitude of defensiveness and usually suspicion.
- Urethral eroticism and/or phallic preoccupation suspected.

NOTES

ROOF

- Fantasy area.

- Intellectual area.

One-dimensional
(Single line connecting two walls)

- Most often observed in mentally deficient who lack capacity to daydream or fantasize.

- Among intellectually normal, may indicate constriction and concrete orientation.

Overly large

- Seeks satisfaction in fantasy.

Peripheral lines faintly drawn

- Feeling control over fantasy is weakening.

- Threatened by intellectual activity.

Peripheral lines heavily drawn

- Overconcern with maintaining control over fantasy.

- Anxiety over intellectual activity.

Poor relation to ground floor

- Poor organization of personality.

ROOF AND CHIMNEY BLOWN DOWN

- Feeling of having been overwhelmed by forces beyond control.

ROOF AND FENCE DRAWN ONLY FOR HOUSE

- Pathological contact with reality, with implication of ego destruction.

ROOF-WALLING

- Suggests the subject lives largely in fantasy.

NOTES

ROOM(S)

- Associations may be aroused by: (1) person usually occupying room; (2) interpersonal relations experienced in room; (3) specific symbolism of room for the subject; (4) function usually associated with room per se or with room by the subject.

- Associations may result in positive or negative feelings regarding room.

- Room's significance needs to be checked by the manner drawn or implied by comments concerning room during drawing or the PDI.

  For functions of room, see *Bathroom, Bedroom, Dining Room, Kitchen, Living Room.*

Paper-chopping of

- Unwillingness to draw room(s) because of unpleasant associations with part of House and/or its customary occupant.

Upper back preferred by subject

- Tendency to withdraw mildly suspected. With other signs of withdrawal significance increases.

View to approach preferred by subject

- Suspicious attitude.

SHRUBS

- Sometimes represent persons.

Drawn haphazardly or along walkway

- Implies mild anxiety at reality level and conscious attempt to channel and control anxiety.

Protectively around House and in profusion

- May symbolize feeling of strong need to construct defensive personality barriers.

NOTES

SHUTTERS
Closed
- Pathoformically or pathologically defensive and withdrawn.

Open
- Can make sensitive adjustment in interpersonal relationships.

SMOKE
Blowing from right to left
- Pessimistic view of future.

Blowing left and right simultaneously
- Pathological reality-testing flaw.

In great profusion
- Considerable inner tension; measured by profusion of smoke.

Single thin line
- Urethral eroticism.
- Felt lack of warmth or emotional stimulation in home.

STEPS, LEADING TO BLANK WALL
- Conflict situation producing reality-testing disability.
- Inaccessibility although subject may wish to deal with people easily and freely.
- Organicity may be suspected.

TRANSPARENT "GLASS BOX"
- Symbolizes feeling of being watched with concomitant desire to exhibit self.

NOTES

TREES

- Frequently represent specific persons.

- If trees seem to shelter House, strong needs for dependency and/or feelings of parental domination are suggested.

VENT STACK PROTRUDING FROM ROOF

- Phallic preoccupation.

- Some positive correlation exists between this sign and enuresis and/or urethral eroticism.

WALKWAY

Narrow at junction with house and broad at end

- Attempt to cloak with superficial friendliness the basic desire to remain aloof.

Very long

- Lessened accessibility, often accompanied by need for more adequate socialization.

WALL(S)

Absence of baseline to

- Poor contact with reality, unless paper-based; feelings of unreality.

Adequacy of

- Directly related to ego strength.

NOTES

WALL(S) (continued)

Baseline to, emphasized
- Anxiety at reality level with implication of difficulty suppressing or repressing oppositional tendencies.

Crumbling
- Disintegrating ego.

Disconnected
- Organicity suspected with possible feelings of loss of control over primitive drives and with feelings of depersonalization.

Double perspective, narrow endwalls
- Sign of organicity.

Double perspective, overly large endwall
- Heightened tendency to protect self.

- Schizophrenia, particularly when center wall is blank.

- Organicity may be a factor.

Horizontal dimension overemphasized
- Temporal disorientation because past and/or future presumed to dominate.

- May be vulnerable to environmental pressure since much of the subject available at reality level for assault.

- Affective disorders and/or latent homosexuality suspected.

Peripheral lines faint and inadequate
- Feeling of impending breakdown; weak ego control.

- Has ceased to struggle against ego threats.

NOTES

WALL(S) (continued)
Peripheral lines overemphasized
- Conscious effort to maintain control.

Single perspective (only one wall shown)
- Serious withdrawal and oppositional tendencies if wall is sidewall.

- Normal for children up to age 8 years, if only front wall; for others represents expression of great need to maintain acceptable facade in interpersonal relations.

Transparent
- Compulsive need to structure situation as much as possible.

- Mental defective if use of interior rather than exterior details; feelings of inadequacy in situations not fully supportive and protective.

- In adult of once-normal intelligence, severe critical judgment or reality-testing flaw.

- Often associated with organicity.

Vertical dimension overemphasized
- Satisfaction sought in fantasy; less contact with reality than desirable.

WALL AND ROOF
Peripheral boundaries of
- Peripheral boundaries of personality with character of line indicating flexibility and strength thereof.

Together
- Ego boundary. Method of presentation determines ego strength.

NOTES

WINDOW(S)

- Modes of contact, less direct and immediate than door(s).

Absence of

- Hostility, withdrawal.

Absent from ground floor

- Hostility, withdrawal.

Absent from upper story but present on ground floor

- Serious gap between reality and fantasy.

Bathroom

- Conventionally smallest window drawn.

- When overemphasized, reflects experiences involving severe toilet training during childhood, masturbation guilt, and/or compulsive handwashing.

Curtained

- Withdrawal, reserved accessibility.

- If curtains, shades, shutters, etc., not closed, controlled interaction with anxiety is implied.

Emphasized by reinforcement and without much detailing

- Concern over interaction with partial cause for concern being orificial fixation.

Ground floor, last detail drawn

- Distaste for interpersonal contacts.

- Tendency to withdraw from reality.

Living room

- Conventionally largest window drawn.

- When smallest drawn, distaste for social intercourse and for inadequate intrafamilial social relationships.

NOTES

WINDOW(S) (continued)

Many bare

- Behaves bluntly and directly.

- Many windows indicate readiness to make contact. Absence of shades, curtains, etc., implies limited need (no more than average) to mask feelings.

Many curtained

- Anxiety about interaction with environment if drawn significantly.

- If curtains easily and freely drawn, implication is that the subject feels able to make refined relationships within home.

Many panes

- Accessible but reserved.

Open

- If House occupied, very accessible or desires to be so.

- If unoccupied House, weak ego defense.

- In either case may lack control to pathoformic degree.

Outline overemphasized by reinforcement

- Oral fixation or oral character traits.

- Occasionally suggestive of anal fixation.

- Anxiety concerning person associated with room or anxiety within it.

Pane indicated by single, dissecting, vertical line

- Fixation upon female genitals suggested.

Paneless

- Tendency to react bluntly with minimum of tact.

NOTES

WINDOW(S) (continued)

Placement of, lack of conformity from wall to wall and floor to floor
- Organization and form difficulty suggested, which may be early schizophrenia if deviant placement occurs in constellation of many signs of high concept formation, and if one of many gross flaws.
- Organicity a possibility.

Proportion distorted
- Overconcern about relationships to person(s) occupying room represented by window or function emphasized by room.

  See room (*Bathroom, Bedroom, Dining Room, Kitchen, Living Room*).

Triangular
- Overconcern about female sex symbol if window significantly drawn.

With locks
- Hostility, withdrawal.
- Overly fearful of danger from without.

NOTES

Tree

ANIMAL PEEKING FROM HOLE IN TREE
- Feeling that segment of personality is pathoformically free from control and presumably has destructive potentialities; obsessive guilt.

- Children often identify with an animal, thus depicting regressive yearnings for withdrawn, warm, protecting uterine existence.

APPLE TREE
- Frequently drawn by dependent children.

- Pregnant women or those desiring children often draw apple trees.

APPLES, FALLING OR FALLEN
- Indicates child's feeling of rejection.

BARK
Depicted by vine-like vertical lines well separated
- Suggests schizoid characteristics.

Easily drawn
- Well-balanced interaction.

Inconsistently or heavily drawn
- Anxiety.

Meticulously drawn
- Compulsiveness with overconcern about relationships with environment.

BRANCHES
- Degree of flexibility of branches, number, size, and extent of interrelationship indicate view of adaptability and availability for deriving satisfactions in environment.

NOTES

BRANCHES (continued)

- Degree of ability to reach others or sustain growth in achievement.

Absolute symmetry of

- Implies feelings of ambivalence; inability to grant dominance to emotional or intellectual course of action.

Broken, bent, or dead

- Significant psychic or physical trauma.

- Castration feelings: psychosexual or psychosocial.

Indicated by shaded implication

- When easily and quickly drawn, indicative of tactful but possibly superficial interaction.

Indicated by unshaded implication

- Oppositional tendencies.

Intended to be two dimensional but not "closed" at distal end

- Little control over expression of drives.

New growth protruding from barren trunk

- Reversal of crippling belief that seeking satisfaction from environment was fruitless.

- Probably sexual rejuvenation, if history of impotence exists.

One-dimensional, not forming a system and inadequately joined to a one-dimensional trunk

- Organicity.

- Impotence feelings, futility, lack of ego strength with poor integration of satisfaction-seeking resources.

NOTES

BRANCHES (continued)

One- or two-dimensional, turning inward
- Strong intratensive ruminative tendencies.

Overemphasis to left
- Personality imbalance due to tendency to seek strenuously for immediate, frank emotional satisfaction: extratensivity.

Overemphasis to right
- Personality imbalance produced by strong tendency to avoid or delay emotional satisfaction, or seek satisfaction through intellectual effort. If subject is of dull intelligence, further conflict is self-evident: intratensivity.

Phallic-like
- Sexual preoccupations.
- Strivings for virility.

Spike-like
- Subconscious castration fear.
- Masochistic tendencies if point is at trunk end of branch.

Two-dimensional, drawn like clubs or fingers with little organization
- Strong hostility and aggression.
- If not overtly aggressive, hostility is repressed with considerable inner tension created.

Two-dimensional, partially drawn with relatively refined branch system and foliage by implication
- Implies well-developed ability to deal successfully with people, as in social work.

NOTES

BRANCHES (continued)
"Wrapped" at ends in cloud-like balls
- Inhibitions prevent outward discharge of aggression.

BRANCH STRUCTURE
- Satisfaction obtained from environment.
- Areas of contact with environment.

Abruptly flattened at top
- Attempt to reject or deny painful fantasy life.

In relation to trunk size
See *Tree: Trunk*, p. 87, etc.

Overly large in relation to trunk
- Feeling of basic inadequacy with concomitant overstriving to secure satisfaction from environment.

Tall and narrow
- Tendency to fear seeking satisfaction from and in environment.

DETAILS, ESSENTIAL
- Trunk and one branch may be regarded as normal when the drawing is identified as a stump. Otherwise the drawing may be considered abnormal.

See *Tree: Branches*, p. 67.

GROUND, TRANSPARENCY OF, ROOTS SHOWN BELOW SURFACE
- Pathoformic reality flaw.
- Suggestive of organicity.

NOTES

GROUNDLINE, ARC-LIKE HILL

- Tree upon crest of arc-like hill frequently represents oral-erotic fixation with need for maternal protection.

- When Tree is small, maternal dependence with feelings of isolation and helplessness indicated.

- When Tree is rugged and large, primary implication is strong need for dominance and exhibitionism.

LEAVES
Fallen or falling

- Feels losing ability to hide thoughts and feelings.

- Feels losing ability for more controlled and delicate adjustments in and to environment.

- Feels no longer can conform to society's demands, or no longer appears to conform.

- For females, falling leaves occasionally symbolize menstrual function.

Many presented in detail

- Obsessive-compulsive characteristics.

Need for more

- Need for ability to conceal basic self.

- Need for appearance of conformity.

- Need for means to make more refined adjustments.

Two-dimensional, too large for branches

- Wishes to mask basic feelings of inadequacy with cloak of superficial adjustment.

- Overcompensatory attempt to take flight into reality.

NOTES

MOVEMENT

- Indicative of strong environmental forces.

- The more involuntary, violent, and unpleasant the movement, the greater the presumed pathoformicity.

PERSPECTIVE
Below subject

- Defeatist attitude.

- Tendency toward concretivity.

- Rejection of person represented by Tree.

Partly up a hill

- Feelings of striving.

- Need for shelter and security.

Top of hill, by itself

- Sometimes indicates feeling of superiority.

- Sometimes represents feeling of isolation, concomitant with struggle for autonomy.

- Sometimes symbolic of tense striving toward distant and perhaps unattainable goal.

ROOTS
Dead

- Intrapersonal imbalance or dissolution with suggested pathoformic loss of drive and grasp of reality.

- Obsessive-depressive feelings associated with early life.

Entering ground, overemphasis upon

- Great need to maintain grasp of reality.

- Insecurity.

NOTES

ROOTS (continued)

Talon-like, not penetrating ground surface
- Poor reality contact.

- Paranoid aggressive attitudes suggested.

Thin-lined, making tenuous contact with ground
- Poor reality contact.

Transparent from underground
- Impairment of reality awareness.

- Organicity, particularly in children.

SCARS
- Psychic and/or physical experience regarded traumatically.

SHADOW
- Anxiety-binding factor within conscious level of personality.

- Unsatisfying relationship of psychological past with psychological present.

SUN

Large
- Acute awareness of relationship to authority figure.

Located behind Tree
- Occasionally the subject interprets Tree as a person in environment, standing between the subject and a warmth-giving person he or she seeks, or as one standing protectively between the subject and person from whom he or she wishes to escape.

NOTES

SUN (continued)

Location of

- Relationship of Tree to source of warmth and/or power.

- Frequently symbolizes relationship felt between the subject and dominant environmental figure.

Rays from, focused on Tree

- Feels dominated or needs to be dominated by authority figure.

Seen in north or south

- Signifies little except adequacy of knowledge of sun's trajectory.

Setting

- Feelings of depression.

Tree leaning from

- Inclination to avoid domination by one who makes the subject feel painfully inadequate.

With cloud between it and Tree

- Implies anxious, unsatisfying relationship between the subject and person in environment.

TREE

- Basic self-portrait.

- Subconscious picture of self psychologically.

- Subconscious picture of development, including customary sensitivities and modes of response.

- Psychosexual level and maturity.

- Feeling of intrapersonal balance.

- View of person other than self.

NOTES

TREE (continued)

- Subconscious picture of development, including customary sensitivities and modes of response.

- Psychosexual level and maturity.

- Feeling of intrapersonal balance.

- View of person other than self.

- Arouses associations concerning life role and ability to derive satisfaction from and in environment.

Age of
- Estimate of psychosexual or psychosocial maturity.

Drawn as two one-dimensional trees
- Strongly suggests pathologic dichotomy of affect and intellect.

- Organicity suspected.

Elapsed time since death of
- Duration of maladjustment or disability; long or short.

"Keyhole"
  (Looping line represents branch structure, not closed where it joins trunk, and two vertical lines, open or closed at base, represent trunk)

- Strong hostile impulses.

- Somewhat rigid personality, with much potential for explosive behavior, if base of trunk closed.

Large but contained within page
- Acutely aware of self in environment.

- Likely to attempt to secure satisfaction in activity rather than fantasy.

NOTES

TREE (continued)
Leaning from sun
- Avoids domination by parental or other authority figure; domination determined by angle of leaning and size of sun.

Leaning to left
- Imbalance of personality because of desire to secure frank, immediate, emotional satisfaction in behaving impulsively.

- From temporal standpoint, fixation on past and/or fear of future.

- Placement of Tree to left or right of page's midpoint has same implications but suggests tendency more basic.

Leaning to right
- Imbalance of personality due to fear of frank, emotional expression with concomitant overemphasis upon intellectual satisfactions.

- From temporal point of view, fixation on future and/or desire to forget unhappy past.

- Placement of Tree to left or right of page's midpoint has same implications but suggests tendency more basic.

Leaning toward sun
- Need to be closer to source of warmth.

- If sun overly large, need to be dominated may be indicated.

"Phallic"
(Similar to "Keyhole Tree," characterized by resemblance to phallus because of small branch structure in proportion to trunk)

NOTES

TREE (continued)

- Common for children under 8 years; high negative correlation with age.

- Suggests psychosexual immaturity and/or phallic preoccupations.

Regarded as pencil or crayon drawing
- Rigid, concrete thinking.

Size of
- Feeling of stature or fantasy concerning desired stature in subject's psychological field; behavior may be different.

Small
- Feels inferior and inadequate.

- Desire to withdraw.

Strength of, contradiction between verbal description and drawing
- Pathoformic inattention.

- Vacillant attitude toward person symbolized by Tree.

- Vacillant view of ability to cope with life.

TRUNK
- Feeling of basic power.

Broad at base with rapid diminishing of breadth
- Early environment lacking in warmth and healthful stimulation with resultant cramping effect on personality maturation.

Broken and tip of tree touching ground
- Symbolically expresses feeling of having been

NOTES

TRUNK (continued)

overwhelmed by internal or external forces beyond control.

Dead
- Feels crippling loss of ego control.

Faint lines
- Feeling of lack of ego strength, indecision and inadequacy, accompanied by anxiety.

Large, with small branch structure
- Precarious personality balance because of frustration engendered by inability to satisfy strong basic needs.

- Emotional immaturity or egocentricity.

Leaning to left and then to right
- Tendency at early age to regress and behave impulsively and at later age to overcompensate by strong controls and fixation on future.

Narrower at base than at higher points
- Striving beyond the subject's strength with concomitant implications of possible collapse of ego control.

One-dimensional, with one-dimensional branches that do not form a system
- Organic state suspected.

- Feelings of impotence, futility, and lack of ego strength with poor integration of inadequate satisfaction-seeking resources.

Overly large
- Feelings of environmental constriction with ten-

NOTES

TRUNK (continued)

dency to react aggressively in reality or fantasy; size and type of branch structure help to identify reality or fantasy.

Reinforcement of peripheral lines

- Need to maintain control or personality intactness.

- Employs compensatory defenses to cloak and combat fear of personality diffusion and integration.

Tiny

- Feelings of basic inadequacy and ineptness.

Truncated with tiny branches growing from stump

- Core of self felt to be damaged.

- Stunted growth with renewed efforts or hope for regrowth; observed in early stages of therapy with children.

Two-dimensional, with one-dimensional branches

- Good early development but later interference by serious traumatic events.

Very slender, with large branch structures

- Precarious personality balance because of overstriving for satisfaction.

Width suggests Tree had been much taller

- Acutely traumatic episode in past suggested.

WIND

Blowing from ground level to tree-top

- Compulsive need to escape reality and enter fantasy.

Blowing from subject

- Desire to deny feelings of pressure.

NOTES

WIND (continued)

- Desire to aggress against sources of frustration.

- If the subject feels power to direct wind, frank psychosis with aggressive elements, at least in fantasy, may be suspected.

- If the subject means the wind has stopped blowing toward him or her, environmental situation may be improving.

Blowing from top to bottom

- Compulsive need to escape fantasy and return to reality.

Blowing from Tree toward subject

- Narcissistic tendency; for example, wishes or feels control over person the Tree represents.

Blowing in all directions simultaneously

- Suggestive of acute reality testing failure.

NOTES

Person

ARMS
- Tools to control or change environment.

Absence of
- Strong feeling of inadequacy; cannot cope with problems presented by interpersonal relationships.
- Feeling of futility at continuing struggle; hence, suicidal tendencies may be present.
- Need for self-mutilation.

Broad
- Basic feeling of strength for striving.

Broader at hand than shoulder
- Lack of control of action and compulsivity of action.

Drawn not as integral part of trunk but extended across back of trunk and forward on either side
- Subject finds self doing or having completed acts over which he or she had no control.

Folded across chest
- Suspicious, hostile attitudes.

Held behind back
- Reluctance to meet people halfway.
- Need to control expression of aggressive, hostile drives.

Long and muscular
- Need for compensatory physical prowess.

NOTES

ARMS (continued)

Overly long
- Overambitious striving.

Relaxed and flexible
- Good adjustment to interpersonal strivings.

Tense and held tight to body
- Rigidity.

Thin
- Feelings of weakness and futility of striving.

Very short
- Absence of striving with feelings of inadequacy.
- Castration feelings or fears.

Wing-like
- At times seen in drawings of schizoid subjects.

BEARD
- Phallic symbol of need to demonstrate virility.

BELT, HEAVILY SHADED
- Strong conflict between expression and control of sex and/or other body drives.

BREASTS, OVEREMPHASIS UPON
- Psychosexual deviations, fixations, immaturity.
- Maternal dependence.

BUTTOCKS, OVEREMPHASIS UPON
- Psychosexual deviations, fixations, immaturity.
- Homosexual tendencies if drawn by male.

NOTES

BUTTONS, MULTIPLICITY OF

- Regression to or fixation at oral dependency in adults of average intelligence or higher.

- Strong dependence on mother if in children.

CARTOON-LIKE PERSON

- Self-depreciatory attitude.

CHIN, OVEREMPHASIS UPON

- Feelings of impotence, often more social than sexual.

CHINLINE, ABSENCE OF, IN FULL-FACE PRESENTATION

See *Person: Neck, Baseline, Omission of in Profile*, p. 113.

CLOWN

- Depreciatory attitude toward self or the person represented by the drawing.

DEFORMITY OF PART(S)

- May represent duplication of similar, real deformity of the subject and/or expression of maladjusted reaction to part drawn and its symbol to the subject.

DETAILS, ESSENTIAL

- Head, trunk, two legs, and two arms (unless absence of arm or leg or both arms and legs accounted for verbally or by profile presentations), two eyes, nose, mouth, and two ears (unless absence accounted for verbally or by profile presentation).

NOTES

EARRINGS

- Frequently drawn by subjects with sexual preoccupations of exhibitionist type.

EARS

Absence of

- Suggests auditory hallucinations.

- Sometimes in well-adjusted mental defectives; often in drawings of "normal" young children.

Overemphasis upon

- Possible auditory hallucinations.

- Usually in drawings of subjects acutely sensitive to criticism.

Underemphasis upon

- Desire to shut out criticism.

EYES

Absence of

- Visual hallucinations suspected.

Disproportionately small

- Desire to see as little as possible.

Drawn as closed or concealed by hat brim

- Strong desire to avoid unpleasant visual stimuli.

Drawn as hollow sockets

- Marked reluctance to accept visual stimuli.

- Hostility toward others.

Large with pupils omitted

- Guilt concerning voyeuristic tendencies.

NOTES

FACE, EMPHASIS UPON
- Overconcern about interrelationships or with outward appearances.
- If definite attempt made to give appearance of happiness, the subject probably is acutely aware of need to maintain acceptable facade.

FACIAL FEATURES
- Include eyes, ears, nose, mouth.
- Receptors of external stimuli.
- Sensory contact with reality.

Some masculine and some feminine
- Sexual ambivalence.

FEET
- Index of feelings of mobility, physiological and/or psychological, in interpersonal sphere.

Absence of
- Expression of crippling lack of autonomy.

Disproportionately long
- Need for security.
- Need to demonstrate virility.

Disproportionately tiny
- Constriction, dependence.

On tiptoe
- Tenuous grip of reality.
- Strong need for flight.

Overdetailing of
- Obsessive traits with strong feminine component.

NOTES

FEET (continued)
Pointing in opposite directions
- Highly ambivalent feelings if drawn by subject above average in intelligence.

FINGERS
Absence of
- Feeling of inability to make more refined adjustments to interpersonal problems.

- Self-mutilation wishes due to guilt over masturbation or stealing.

Drawn last
See *Person: Hands, Drawn Last*, p. 107.

Large and spike-like
- Hostility.

One-dimensional and enclosed by loop
- Conscious efforts to suppress aggressive impulses.

HAIR
- Expression of virility and virility striving.

Heavily shaded
- Anxiety over thinking or fantasy.

Long and unshaded
- Highly ambivalent or hostile sex fantasy.

Unshaded, enclosing face in vise-like fashion
- Believes hostile feelings control him or her.

HANDS
- Means for more refined and sensitive adjustments to environment with emphasis upon interpersonal relationships.

NOTES

HANDS (continued)

Absence of

- Feelings of inadequacy.

- Possible feelings of castration.

Drawn in pelvic-defense position

- Defense against sexual approach with fear suggested.

- Preoccupation with sex.

Drawn last

- Marked reluctance to make immediate and intimate environmental contact.

- At times predicated on desire to avoid revealing feelings of inadequacy.

Heavily shaded

- Guilt over manual action or fantasized action (masturbation, assault, theft, etc.).

In pockets

- Controlled evasion, subject to modification, depending on contents of hand or pocket. At times represents compulsive masturbatory activity.

Overly large

- Strong need for refined adjustments in social intercourse with feelings of inadequacy and tendency to behave impulsively in such situations.

HEAD

- Area of intelligence and control.

- Area of fantasy.

Aversion of

- Implies evasion and withdrawal; at times, guilt.

NOTES

HEAD (continued)
- Desire to determine terms on which the subject will be accessible.

Emphasis upon peripheral lines of
- Strong efforts to maintain control in face of disturbing fantasy or possibly obsessive or delusional behavior.

Large
- Subconscious stress on believed importance of role of mentation in life.
- Emphasis on fantasy as source of satisfaction.

Small
- In drawings of obsessive-compulsives.
- Wish to deny intellectual control which prevents satisfaction of body impulses (Machover, 1949).
- Obsessive subject's expression of desire to deny site of painful thoughts and guilt feelings.
- Feelings of intellectual inadequacy.

With back to viewer
- Pathognomonic of paranoid-schizoid withdrawal.

KNEES, EMPHASIS UPON
- Suggests homosexual tendencies.

LEGS
Absence of
- Pathological feelings of constriction.
- Castration feelings.

Broad-based stance
- Defiance and/or insecurity.

NOTES

LEGS (continued)
Crossed
- Defense against sexual approach.

Disparity in size
- Ambivalence over strivings for autonomy.

Disproportionately long
- Strong need and/or striving for autonomy.

Disproportionately short
- Feelings of physiological and/or psychological immobility.

Held tightly together
- Rigidity and tension.

- Possible sexual maladjustment.

MOUTH
Overemphasis upon
- Psychosexual deviations, fixations, immaturity. Often expressive of guilt feelings and/or anxiety occasioned by oral-erotic or oral-aggressive impulses.

  See *Person: Facial Features*, p. 103.

Overly large
- Oral eroticism.

MOVEMENT
- The more violent, unpleasant, and involuntary the movement, the greater the presumed pathoformicity.

NOTES

MUSCLES, OVEREMPHASIZED WITH LITTLE CLOTHING
- Suggests "body narcissism" and schizoid tendency by self-absorbed individuals (Machover, 1949).

MUSTACHE
- Phallic symbol.

NECK

- Organ joining control area (head) and impulse area (body); thus is an index of coordination of these two areas.

Absence of
- Helpless before body drives which frequently overwhelm the subject.

Baseline, omission of in profile
- Unhappily free flow of basic body drives with probable lack of adequate control.

Long and thin
- Schizoid characteristic.

One-dimensional
- Poor coordination between body drives and intellectual control.

Sequence disturbed
- Conflict between control and expression of emotion.

NOSE, OVEREMPHASIS UPON
- Phallic preoccupation.
- Possibly castration fear.
- Sexual maladjustment presumed greater if nose is turned up in full-face presentation and particularly if placed above eyes.

NOTES

PAPER-SIDING
- Basic general insecurity with, at times, more specific temporal insecurity.

PELVIC CLOSURE INCOMPLETE
- Well-developed sexual conflict.
- Strong homosexual tendencies; guilt and anxiety suspected.

PERSON
- Impression of the subject psychologically and/or physiologically.
- As the subject would like to be.
- Attitudes toward interpersonal relationships.
- Attitudes toward specific interpersonal relationship.
- Specific fears, obsessive beliefs, etc.
- Person in environment the subject most likes.
- Person in environment the subject most dislikes.
- Person toward whom the subject has ambivalent feelings.

Clothed carefully
- Clothing or social narcissism in infantile, egocentric subjects.

Controlled running
- Need to escape or achieve.

Marked proportional differences in right and left sides
- Sexual role confusion.
- Personality imbalance.

NOTES

PERSON (continued)
Mutilated
- Rejection of Person or symbol of whole, part, or parts mutilated.

Nude
- If sexual parts displayed, may be expressing rebellion against society or awareness of sexual conflicts.

- May be expressing body narcissism; found in infantile, egocentric subjects.

Running blindly
- May experience panic states at times.

Stick figure
- Frequently drawn by psychopaths and those who find interpersonal relationships distasteful.

- Organicity suspected.

Walking easily
- Good adjustment.

POCKETS PLACED AT BREASTS
- Oral and affectional deprivation usually found in infantile and dependent subjects.

- Psychosexual identification with mother.

PROFILE
Absolute
- Serious withdrawal and oppositional tendencies.

Ambivalent
(Instances when part of body faces opposite direction from other body parts)

NOTES

PROFILE (continued)
- Indicates extreme frustration with strong desire to abandon very unsatisfactory situation.

SHOULDERS
Inequality of size
- Personality imbalance.

Overly large
- Feelings of great strength or overconcern about the need for strength or power.

Sharply squared
- Overdefensive, hostile attitudes.

Size of
- Index of feeling of basic physical strength or power.

Tiny
- Feelings of inferiority.

Well-drawn and neatly rounded
- Implies smooth, flexible, well-balanced expression of power.

TEETH PROMINENTLY PRESENTED
- Aggression, usually oral only.

TIE, OVEREMPHASIS UPON
- Phallic preoccupation with feelings of impotency suspected.

TRUNK
- Seat of basic needs and drives.

NOTES

TRUNK (continued)
Absence of
- Denial of body drives.

Long and narrow
- Schizoid characteristic.

Overly large
- Presence of many unsatisfied drives which the subject acutely feels.

Unusually small
- Denial of body drives and/or feelings of inferiority.

WAISTLINE
- Coordinator of power drives (upper trunk) and sex drives (lower trunk).

Overemphasis upon
- Strong conflict between expression and control of sex drives.

WITCH
- Hostility toward females expressed overtly in punitive fashion.

NOTES

CHAPTER 2
POST-DRAWING INTERROGATION (PDI)

House

1. Does that house have an upstairs?

This question helps to appraise the subject's reality level (e.g., when the subject replies "No" but two floors are clearly indicated by the placement of the windows in the drawing).

Sometimes the subject will indicate that there is an upstairs to the House when only one floor of windows is shown. If this floor could be the upstairs according to the drawing, then the subject has a need to omit the first floor windows, thus revealing a reluctance to make social contact or the need to avoid reality.

Conversely, if the lower floor is depicted in the drawing, then the subject has a serious gap between fantasy life and reality. He or she may also be indicating considerable guilt regarding fantasies, thus the denial in the drawing of the existence of the upper floor.

2. Is that your house? (If not) Whose house is it?

This question determines whether the subject is consciously identifying the drawn House with his or her home or with someone else's house. If it is someone else's house, the clinician must determine through the drawing and subsequent PDI responses whether this is a positive or negative association. Often the association of the drawn House with someone else's will indicate a rejection of one's own home and a preference for someone else's home.

Sometimes an attachment to a previous house in which the subject lived is brought out by this question. On the other hand, it could reveal the improved home situation which is

NOTES

presently being experienced as compared to prior home conditions.

3. Would you like to own that house? Why?

A positive reply reveals a positive feeling towards the House; a negative answer reveals rejection of the House.

If the subject prefers this House to his or her own because "it is bigger," the clinician can suspect either actual overcrowdedness in the present home or a feeling of frustration there.

If the House is rejected because it is too large, the subject very likely feels insecure in his or her home.

4. a. Which room would you take for your own?

This question is usually interpreted to mean which bedroom would be wanted. Any other selection may be regarded as significant and can be interpreted in terms of the significance of the particular room selected.

The position of the room selected with respect to the other bedrooms can indicate the degree of closeness felt towards each member of the family. When the room selected is farther from the parents' room than the room of a sibling, the indications are that the subject feels the sibling to be closer to the parents than he or she is.

If the subject chooses a room upstairs, especially in the rear of the House, he or she is indicating a desire to withdraw. Sometimes a room upstairs is selected so that the subject can see outside more easily; this indicates some degree of fearfulness and possibly some paranoid feelings.

Occasionally the reasons for selecting a room downstairs will reveal feelings of insecurity and possibly a need to be closer to reality.

4. b. Whom would you like to have live in that house with you?

The reply will indicate the family members, if any, with

NOTES

whom the subject maintains emotional ties. The clinician can assume that the subject rejects those not chosen.

5. As you look at that house, does it seem to be close by or far away?

"Close by" indicates attainability and/or feeling of warmth and welcome.

"Far away" indicates that the subject feels rejected or is rejecting someone, or may indicate a feeling of inaccessibility or of inability to cope with his or her home.

If the drawing appears to be the reverse of the response, a serious reality flaw may be present.

6. Does it seem to be above you, below you, or about even with you?

"Above" suggests a feeling either of rejection by home or of striving towards a home situation which the subject is not likely to attain. This reply often indicates overstriving because of unreasonable demands being made at home. Then, too, it might reveal the desire to withdraw and to make only limited contact with other persons.

"Below" usually reveals rejection of the home or, less significantly, rejection of the common tendency to glorify the home. Likewise, the subject may feel above the usual emotional and restrictive home ties.

7. What does that house make you think of?

Following are some sample responses and their interpretations:

"A fork" reveals unrealistic thinking, since there is no remote resemblance between the drawing of the House and a fork. This could also be interpreted as a hostile, evasive answer.

"Makes me feel good" is a wish about the home rather than a fact based on this subject's history.

"A nice little house" expresses satisfaction with the home.

"That it is going to fall" expresses anticipation of ego

NOTES

collapse.

"A half-built house" indicates that the subject feels incomplete, thus reflecting poor self-concept.

"Being at home" shows a preference for being at home where the subject feels secure and where dependent needs are met. The subject encounters stress in interpersonal relations outside the home.

"When I ain't got nobody to play with when I go home" obviously indicates a lack of playmates in the immediate neighborhood.

"Our gardener," with further questioning, revealed the subject's close, warm relationship with the family's gardener when they lived in a foreign country.

"Skyscraper" reveals the impersonal atmosphere of the home.

"A cold day" reveals the lack of warmth in the family.

"Looks lonely" reflects identification with the house; the lack of friends was also expressed.

"I want to go home" is a very simplistic statement of the child's desire to be at home instead of amid the frustrations at school.

"A shelter" is all the home means to this child.

"A new house," along with the other PDI responses, reveals clearly the desire to be with some other father and mother.

"A barn" expresses hostility towards the home.

8. Is that a happy, friendly sort of house?

If "No," the subject tends to indicate the unhappy and/or unfriendly atmosphere within the home. Of course, the clinician must consider the possibility that the subject may identify the House with some home other than his or her own.

9. What is the weather like in this picture?

The degree of stress, if any, or the degree of warmth within the home is revealed.

NOTES

10. Which person that you know does that house make you think of?

The reply to this question helps in the interpretation of the total record in that the examiner has an idea as to how the subject is identifying the House.

11. Has anyone or anything ever hurt that house? (If so) How?

This reveals possible traumatic experiences that the subject has had and the degree to which the ego has been damaged by these environmental attacks on his or her personality.

12. Suppose this sun were some person you know—who would it be?

This helps to determine persons identified as a source of warmth and/or authority (especially when the sun is quite large).

13. What does that house need most? Why?

Some responses can be interpreted in symbolism with the drawn House representing the subject or the subject's home; others can be taken literally. The total H-T-P picture and case history can help the examiner to make such decisions.

Following are some sample responses and their interpretations:

"Somebody to clean it up" indicates a need for help in changing or improving oneself to be rid of problems.

"A door and more windows and bedrooms" indicates frustration in the home because of the need for more room.

"More bushes in the yard" shows a need for a more structured environment.

"Windows" reflects the need for more social interaction.

"A chimney" indicates that this male subject is aware of his castration feelings and would like to develop his masculinity.

NOTES

"Upstairs in it" reflects acute awareness of intellectual difficulties; recognized need for intelligence.

"Strong wood to keep it standing and enough people living in it" shows the need for a strong ego with which to cope with environmental pressures and the desire to improve the social life within the home.

"Point" shows a need to make a better impression upon others.

"Taken care of" indicates that the subject feels neglected and wants the parents to give more attention.

"Cement" is another way of indicating a need for more ego strength.

"Dirt so it will stay in the ground" shows awareness of the need to maintain contact with reality.

"Roof" reflects the subject's feeling that he or she needs a new brain to be able to learn in school.

"Keep people in it comfortable" points to uncomfortableness in the home situation.

"Food" can be taken literally for a subject who comes from a poverty-stricken home. In other cases it would indicate oral needs.

"Summer" indicates a need for more warmth at home.

"Fence around it for protection" expresses a need to withdraw in order to protect oneself from the environment.

14. Where does that chimney lead to in the house?

When a disturbance is noted in the manner in which the chimney is drawn, this question can often associate this disturbance with a given person in the home or a particular aspect of home life by denoting the room to be associated with the chimney.

NOTES

Tree

1. What kind of tree is that?

"Apple tree" is often obtained from dependent subjects.

"Willow tree," referring to the "weeping willow," is often produced by individuals who are depressed.

Other trees do not seem to have particular significance in a general sense, although there may be personal meanings for certain subjects. There is some indication that oak trees may be indicative of a feeling of strength, and "Christmas trees" tend to imply immaturity in older children.

2. Where is that tree?

Replies to this question usually have little significance. They sometimes reveal associations with past homes or communities which the subject prefers to his or her present location.

3. About how old is that tree?

This may be an indication of the subject's estimate of his or her psychosexual and/or psychosocial maturity.

4. Is that tree alive?

A response indicating the Tree is dead reveals a feeling of utter futility. On a few occasions it has been known to be associated with feelings of guilt.

5. A. a. What is there about that tree which makes you think it's alive?

This generally helps to appraise the subject's reality level.

5. A. b. Is any part of the tree dead? Which part?

NOTES

A branch which is dead may signify one or more of the following: (1) psychic or physical trauma; (2) castration feelings, either psychosexual or psychosocial; (3) loss of satisfaction-seeking resources. If psychic or physical trauma, location of the dead branch is likely to indicate the age at which the trauma occurred. To determine this age, consider the distance from the bottom to the top of the Tree to represent the subject's life span. For example, if the dead branch is located two-thirds of the way from the bottom to the top and the subject's age is 9 years, then the trauma is estimated to have occurred at age 6.

Roots described as dead may indicate: (1) intrapersonal imbalance or dissolution with suggested pathoformic loss of drive and grasp of reality; (2) obsessive-depressive feelings associated with early life.

A dead trunk indicates awareness of a crippling loss of ego control.

Dead leaves may indicate inability to make more controlled and delicate adjustments to the environment.

5. A. c. What do you think caused it to die?

Death caused by parasites, worms, disease, wind, etc., indicates that something extrapersonal is blamed for the subject's maladjustment.

Death cause by rotting of roots, trunk, and/or limbs indicates that the subject feels that it is his or her inner self which is unwholesome and unacceptable.

5. B. a. What do you think caused it (the tree) to die?

See above (Question 5. A. c.).

5. B. b. Will it ever be alive again?

Sometimes the subject will say that the Tree is dead when he or she really means that it is bare of leaves because it is winter. This question is designed to determine if this is the intent. If so, the fact that the Tree is "dead" has no significance.

NOTES

6. Does that tree look more like a man or a woman to you?

More often than not this question brings out identification of the Tree with either the father (man) or mother (woman). Occasionally the sex of the Tree may indicate the sex of some other individual with whom the subject identifies.

In rare instances the response indicates sexual identification. When this is true, it is usually on a deep-seated level.

7. If that tree were a person, which way would that person be facing?

The direction the Tree is facing represents the attitude toward the subject by the person the subject identifies with the Tree. Therefore, if the Tree is identified as a woman and facing toward the subject, it is likely that the subject feels accepted by his or her mother. If the Tree is identified as a man, it would indicate acceptance by the father.

If the Tree is facing away from the subject, complete rejection by the father or mother is indicated. If the Tree is facing to the subject's right or left, the rejection is less complete.

Although the subject usually refers to a parental figure in reply to this question, there are occasions when he or she is expressing the attitude towards him or her by someone other than a parent.

8. Is that tree by itself or in a group of trees?

If the Tree is said to be by itself, there is a likelihood that the subject experiences social isolation among peers. There are occasional exceptions which can usually be detected through other channels on the H-T-P itself.

Usually the response "in a group of trees" is not significant. Occasionally it might connote strong feelings of domination by others.

If the subject indicates that the Tree would like to be by itself, asocial tendencies are likely.

NOTES

9. Looking at that tree, does it seem above you, below you, or about even with you?

If "above," overstriving is likely, but it may also suggest a desire to seek satisfactions in fantasy.

If "below," the subject may feel inferior, have a defeatist attitude, manifest a tendency towards concretivity, or harbor a rejecting attitude towards the person represented by the Tree.

If the answer is contrary to what is depicted in the drawing, there can be some question as to the ability to be realistic.

10. What is the weather like in this picture?

This question is designed to determine the view of one's environment in general. Stormy weather indicates a great deal of environmental stress. The hot-cold continuum gives a clue as to the degree of warmth experienced. If raining, obviously the subject does not view the environment with the degree of satisfaction that he or she would if it were warm and clear.

11. What kind of weather do you like best?

The reply to this question helps to interpret reactions to the other questions about the weather. Obviously cold weather would not have the same significance to a person who preferred it to warm weather as it would to those who like warm weather best. A rather large number of children prefer snow to any other because they like to play in the snow.

12. Is any wind blowing in this picture?

This is to determine the extent to which the subject experiences environmental pressures.

13. Show me which way the wind is blowing.

"Left to right" is a healthy sign, indicating an ability to cope with the pressures experienced.

NOTES

"Right to left" indicates an ego which is too weak to cope with environmental pressure; tendency to regress under pressure.

If the subject feels the power to direct the wind, a frank psychosis with aggressive elements, at least in fantasy, may be suspected.

If the subject means that the wind has stopped blowing towards him or her, the environmental situation may be improving.

"From ground level to tree-top" reflects a compulsive need to escape reality and enter fantasy.

"From top to bottom" reflects a compulsive need to escape fantasy and return to reality.

"Towards me" is a narcissistic tendency; perhaps a wish to feel control over the person the Tree represents.

"In all directions simultaneously" is suggestive of acute reality-testing failure.

14. What sort of wind is it?

The reply gives a clue to the degree of pressure experienced.

15. Suppose this sun were some person you know—who would it be?

The response identifies a source of warmth or a source of domination (if the drawn sun is quite large).

16. Of what does that tree make you think?

This is chiefly a question which produces some association. The responses must be interpreted in that light.

17. Is it a healthy tree?

A negative reply may indicate concern about one's own health or the health of a person associated with the Tree. It may

NOTES

also be indicative of the possibility of psychosomatic complaints. A person who complains about his or her health but gives no affirmative answer to this question is more likely to be a malingerer than to have a truly psychosomatic condition.

18. Is it a strong tree?

Although this may pertain to physical strength, more often it is an indication of the subject's view of his or her ego strength.

19. Of which person you know does that tree remind you?

This gives more opportunity to indicate an individual with whom the subject is identified. Often this helps to clarify the response to Question 6.

20. Has anyone or anything ever hurt that tree? (If so) How?

The purpose of this question is to determine the degree to which a person has experienced environmental attacks upon his or her personality. The part of the tree damaged can offer some insight as to how these attacks are affecting the subject.

If a branch or branches are broken, bent, or dead, there is likely to have been a psychic or physical trauma in the subject's past. Location of the branch on the tree can give some indication as to the age at which the trauma occurred (see Question 5. A. b.). This may also be indicative of castration feelings, either psychosexual or psychological.

A broken trunk may indicate the subject's having been overwhelmed by forces beyond his or her control. Otherwise, damage to the trunk or bark of the Tree could indicate damage to the ego which may affect control and/or ability to cope with pressures.

Damage to the roots of the Tree tends to indicate a weakening of the grip upon reality; the environmental attacks may be forcing the subject to attempt to escape from a painful reality.

NOTES

21. What does that tree need most? Why?

Very frequently answers include sunshine and/ or water and, therefore, they should not be regarded as particularly significant. Other replies can be interpreted as representing or symbolizing the subject's own needs.

NOTES

Person

1. Is that a man, woman, boy, or girl?

The reply gives a clue to the subject's sexual identification. When the subject gives a sex which is quite different from the drawing, either the reality level is poor or there might be guilt feelings concerning actual sexual identification. Actual identification would be represented by the drawing itself (see *Person: Person*, p. 115).

The sex given may indicate the sex the subject would like to be even though the sexual identification may be otherwise.

2. How old is he (she)?

The degree to which the age given matches the drawing gives a clue to reality level. It may indicate the age which the subject would like to be, the age of the person with whom the subject is identifying, or the age of the drawn Person as viewed by the subject (when no particular identification is made).

When the given age is younger than the subject, it could indicate a regressive trend in that the subject would like to be younger than he or she really is. On the other hand, it may indicate the felt degree of social and/or emotional maturity.

3. Who is he (she)?

4. Who is that?

These two questions are designed to pinpoint the identification of the drawn Person. When this identification is quite different from the sex and/or age given, the clinician can suspect a somewhat defensive associative process in the subject's thinking. This may be confirmed in replies to other questions.

This identification may indicate the person with whom the subject is identified, likes, or dislikes. The total picture will help

NOTES

to determine which of these meanings to apply in a specific instance.

5. What is he (she) doing?

6. Where is he (she) doing it?

Question 6 is rarely significant. When it is, its significance will usually be apparent to the examiner.

The following are some examples of significant replies to Question 5:

"Going to school" usually indicates preoccupation with school in a positive way. It can also have a negative connotation, in which case it may represent awareness of pressures to do well in school or preoccupation with school problems.

"Getting his picture taken" tends to indicate narcissism or self-centeredness.

"Watching somebody play" represents the subject's social isolation (i.e., tendency to remain aloof of socialization on the school playground).

"He's laughing at me" could indicate sensitivity regarding the opinion others have of him or her, but in this particular case it brought out the need to get the attention of others through behavior mechanisms.

"Just walking around in the woods" represents the child's lack of goal direction; just going through school aimlessly without adequate motivation.

"Teaching karate" brings forth the hostility and need for aggression.

"She's mad 'cause her mother spanked her" brings out the conflict between the subject and her mother.

"Running to get his bicycle because I'm riding it" brings out the subject's conflict with his brother whom he had identified with the drawn Person.

"Getting mad; somebody hit her" brings out the subject's hostility towards her peers because of their attacks upon her.

"Worrying because she's going to lose all her friends"

NOTES

brings out difficulties in interpersonal relationships and the rejection experienced.

"Working in the garage" expresses the subject's interest in his father's activities.

"Looking in the mirror" indicates narcissism.

"Standing looking at me" expresses the subject's sensitivity of the opinion of others toward him. This could also be a narcissistic type of response.

"Filled with joy" is a form of evasion and brings out a hostile attitude.

"My father is taking a picture of him (subject's brother)" expresses jealousy of the affection the father has for the brother.

"Walking her dog" expresses attachment to a dog as a compensatory measure for the lack of affection experienced with parents and peers.

"Sitting in a chair" brings out one of the subject's major school problems: sitting still in the classroom. It also brings out a poor reality level, since the drawn Person is definitely not seated.

"Just standing looking at something, seeing how strange it is" brings to the surface the subject's anxiety.

"Holding hands and going to ask mother if he and her could have something to eat" indicates emotional immaturity and oral needs.

"Just standing outside waiting for a friend to come out and play" expresses a need for playmates.

"Work with me in a book" expresses a need for help with school work.

"Running to the river" expresses a need to escape environmental stress.

"Picking some flowers for his mother" expresses a need to win the mother's affection which has been denied the subject thus far.

"Getting his picture taken after the game" indicates a need for recognition and feeling important.

"(A soldier) watching the gate" expresses a need to be on the defensive, and perhaps paranoid attitudes toward people.

NOTES

"Standing—staring at a girl" reveals precocious sex interest.

"Smiling at me" expresses a desire for father's approval.

7. What is he (she) thinking about?

This generally indicates things which tend to preoccupy the subject's thoughts. They may be positive or negative. The meaning of the response to this question is generally self-explanatory.

When the subject says, "I don't know" or "Nothing," he or she is evading the issue and wants to withhold this information from the examiner.

Occasionally the response may be symbolic and may lend itself to a Freudian or similar type of interpretation.

8. How does he (she) feel? Why?

The response to this question is usually an index of the subject's placement on the continuum of good to poor health or elated-depressive moods. There are times when the response "happy" is merely an evasive reaction. The examiner's clinical judgment can usually determine this.

When the answer is "sick," it may be indicative of psychosomatic complaints and often helps to differentiate between a psychosomatic condition and mere malingering when there has been a history of unexplained illness.

When the reply is "mad" or "mean," the subject is indicating the presence of hostility. Other similar responses can have very obvious meanings (e.g., "lonely," "disliked," "inadequate").

9. What does that person make you think of?

Responses to this question may give clues to self-concept, identification, attitude towards the person represented by the drawing, or what the subject would like to be.

NOTES

Failure to give a meaningful response (i.e., "Nothing" or "I don't know") can indicate either evasiveness or a general inability to identify with anyone.

10. Is that person well?

The healthy reply, of course, is "yes." A "no" response may be indicative of concern about health and could indicate psychosomatic complaints. This question will rarely be answered "yes" by a subject who has a psychosomatic condition, but often will be by malingerers.

11. Is that person happy?

A "yes" response may be a healthy response or may merely be evasive. A "no" response indicates at least some depression in mood tone and will usually occur in depressed individuals.

12. What is the weather like in this picture?

This describes the subject's view of his or her environment with particular emphasis on interpersonal relationships. If it is storming, the response expresses the degree of stress experienced in interpersonal relationships. Responses such as "cold" or "winter" generally indicate a lack of warmth experienced in interpersonal relationships. "Warm" or "sunny" indicates a feeling of warmth associated with people in general or in relationship with the person identified with the drawing. Occasionally these may be evasive replies.

13. Of which person you know does this person remind you? Why?

The reply can give a clue as to identification. The subject may have either positive or negative feelings toward this person; the drawing and the response to this question may help to clarify this point.

NOTES

The reply may give a clue as to self-concept.

14. What kind of clothing is this person wearing?

This question mainly offers some evaluation of reality level.

There may be indications of castration feelings if the sex organs are not present on a nude Person; it might also indicate guilt feelings regarding sex.

15. What does that person need most?

The primary objective is to determine felt need (e.g., love, friends, better clothes, a father).

16. Has anyone ever hurt that person?

Replies to this question will tend to indicate whether the subject has had any traumatic experiences in social relationships. In children it often reveals whether the subject has been picked on by peers (e.g., "Kids threw rocks at him").

17. Suppose that sun were some person you know—who would it be?

This usually indicates with whom the subject identifies warmth or overdomination. For children, inability to identify a parental figure with the sun indicates a lack of warmth in parental relationships with the child. Also, delinquents rarely identify a parent with the sun.

"God," "Jesus," etc., are evasive responses.

Again, inability to identify any person with the sun usually reveals a lack of identification with anyone.

NOTES

CHAPTER 3
THE CHROMATIC PHASE
(The Crayon Drawings)

General Interpretations

BLACK
- Conventionally used for smoke, outlines of the three wholes, hair, shoes, fences, etc.
- Depression of mood tone, the degree of the depression varying directly with the quantity and intensity of its use.
- Anxiety may also be indicated.

BLENDING OR FUSION
- Superior use of color; signifies emotional maturity.
- When the blending is bizarre or very unrealistic, serious emotional disturbance is likely.

BLUE
- Conventionally used for sky, clothing, eyes, curtains.
- Some depression of mood tone.
- Need to exercise control.

BLUE-BLACK COMBINATION
- Schizo-affective type reaction.

BLUE-GREEN
- Conventionally used for distant landscape, sky, dress, sweater, curtains.
- Need for control to maintain security.

NOTES

BROWN

- Conventionally used for trunk of Tree, wall of House, hair, clothing.

COLOR, SIGNIFICANCE OF

- If used conventionally and/or realistically, it has no pathoformic or pathological significance. Color becomes more significant as conventionality and realism are lessened.

- Specific interpretations should be used with great caution. For specific interpretations, see *Black, Blue*, etc.

- The slower, more difficult, and more indecisive the subject's selection of color, the greater the likelihood of personality disturbance.

CRAYON USED AS PENCIL ONLY

- Subject is at least emotionally shy.

- Strong oppositional tendencies with potential for aggression which may be directed externally.

- Lack of emotional depth; common with very young and retarded children.

DISPARITY OF QUALITY BETWEEN CRAYON AND PENCIL DRAWINGS

- The clinician should keep in mind that the chromatic drawings reach a deeper level of personality than do the achromatic drawings. Therefore, there may be a better prognosis when the crayon wholes are superior to the pencil drawings and a worse prognosis when the opposite is true.

GREEN

- Conventionally used for female clothing, sweaters, roof, tree foliage, grass.

NOTES

GREEN (continued)

- Attempt to produce feelings of security or relative freedom from threat.

GREEN-BLACK COMBINATION

- Suggests schizoid affective reaction pattern.

ORANGE

- Conventionally used for oranges, sweaters.

- Pathoformic combination of sensuality and hostility when used deviantly.

- Frequently implies ambivalent attitudes.

PURPLE

- Conventionally used for curtains, minor items of female clothing such as a scarf or kerchief.

- Strong need for power.

RED

- Conventionally used for chimney, lips, hair, apples, cherries, brick house.

- Most sensuous color; erotic color.

- Need for warmth and/or affection.

RED-ORANGE

- Conventionally used for sweaters, dresses.

- Ambivalent feelings for loved object represented or object from whom love is craved.

ROSE-PINK

- Conventionally used for exposed body parts, pencil drawing of person, female clothing.

- Suggests reduced affective response in situations suggested by drawing.

NOTES

SHADING

Extensive in foreground and background

- Presence of much anxiety at reality level.
- Could suggest inferior affect control.
- May indicate deep affect tone.

Spilling over peripheral lines

- Tendency to respond impulsively to additional stimulation.

WHITE

- Never used conventionally.
- Indicative of antisocial attitudes.

WHOLES MUCH LARGER THAN PENCIL DRAWINGS

- Often indicates a tendency for subject to overreact to excitement such as would be created by group situations.
- If size of colored whole is more nearly normal than the pencil drawing, the subject may be more responsive and less withdrawn when experiencing warmth.

YELLOW

- Conventionally used for sun, flowers.
- Strong implications of hostile attitudes.

For entire drawing

- Strong feelings of hostility toward that represented by whole in which it appears.

YELLOW-GREEN

- Conventionally used for landscape, grass.
- Hostile feelings usually expressed in subtle manner.

NOTES

YELLOW-ORANGE

- Conventionally used for sweaters.

- Ambivalent feelings toward love object about to be dissolved in the direction of hostility.

NOTES

House

AREAS COMMONLY SHADED

- Chimney and roof most frequently shaded with color. When other areas are shaded and these are not, the examiner should explore the reasons.

CHIMNEY SHADED BLACK

- Phallic anxiety.

- Depression concerning intimate relations with person associated with the room to which the chimney leads.

DOOR SHADED OR DRAWN WITH YELLOW

- Hostility towards those who try to make the subject socially accessible.

HOUSE

All red

- Much need for affection at home.

All white

- Intense hostility towards home as well as antisocial attitudes.

All yellow

- Intense hostility towards home.

NUMBER OF COLORS

- Well-adjusted subjects use neither less than two nor more than five colors.

- Seven or eight colors indicate the subject is highly labile at best.

- Use of only one color indicates either a fear of emotional stimulation at home or a shallow emotional tone, if only one color is also used for the Tree and the Person.

NOTES

ROOF
Black
- Depression and/or anxiety induced by fantasies or intellectual difficulties.

Blue
- Mild depression of mood tone because of fantasies or intellectual difficulties.

Red
- Erotic fantasies.

White
- Intense oppositional tendencies directed towards fantasies; subject cannot accept or face his or her fantasies.
- Antisocial attitudes which may be internalized through fantasy or which may be induced by intellectual activity.

Yellow
- Hostile fantasies or hostility towards intellectual activities.

WALLS, YELLOW
- Hostility towards home. Hostile behavior may be used as an ego defense mechanism.

WINDOW(S)
Of different colors
- Often the general meaning of the color can be applied to the relationship between the subject and the person associated with a specific window or room. For example, if a red window is known to be the mother's bedroom, the subject has a need for affection from the mother.

NOTES

WINDOW(S) (continued)

Shaded yellow to depict light within
- Implies a feeling that the environment is hostile or activities must be concealed from critical persons.

NOTES

Tree

BRANCHES
Outlined and/or shaded brown
- Conventional use for brown.

- Any other color used in this way may be regarded as pathoformic at least.

Outlined and/or shaded colors other than brown
See specific color used (*Tree, Outlined and/or Shaded with Orange*, etc.).

- In the case of branches, the meaning of the color is probably applied to satisfaction-seeking resources rather than to the environment in general.

BRANCH STRUCTURE SHADED YELLOW-GREEN
- Subject may obtain satisfaction from environment by being hostile in subtle ways.

FOLIAGE SHADED BLUE-GREEN
- Need to maintain control in order to feel secure and to derive adequate satisfaction from environment.

FRUIT PRESENTED IN MANY DIFFERENT COLORS
- Emotional immaturity.

- A tendency to respond with inappropriate affect may be present.

- Obsessive-compulsive traits may be present.

NUMBER OF COLORS
- Well-adjusted subjects use neither less than two nor more than four colors.

- When five or more colors are used, at best subject is highly labile. An exception is when the subject

NOTES

NUMBER OF COLORS (continued)

presents a realistic blending of colors to represent the changing of colors in the fall. In this usage of color, mature affect is indicated.

TREE

Black used as pencil drawing

- Relatively common among the mentally retarded but not as healthy as the use of brown for this purpose.

- At best indicates shallow emotional tone.

- May indicate hostility with concomitant anxiety.

Outlined and/or shaded with orange

- Ambivalent attitudes toward that which is symbolized by the Tree.

Outlined and/or shaded with orange-yellow

- Ambivalent attitudes toward that which is symbolized by the Tree with a valence towards hostility.

Outlined and/or shaded with red-orange

- Ambivalent attitudes toward that which is symbolized by the Tree with a valence towards love. A healthier sign than orange or orange-yellow.

Outlined and/or shaded with white

- Intense oppositional tendencies directed towards subject's environment in general.

- May indicate intense hostility towards person symbolized by Tree.

- Antisocial attitudes and delinquency or potential delinquency.

NOTES

TREE (continued)
Outlined and/or shaded with yellow
- Intense hostility towards environment and/or person symbolized by Tree.

TRUNK
Outlined with black, heavy lines
- Overly anxious about maintaining control and may be depressed because of weak ego.

Shaded with black
- Anxiety and/or depression concerning weak ego.

Shaded with black and brown combination
- This suggests an ability to react on a mature level and is essentially a healthy sign.

Shaded with green
- A need to cover up weak ego by behaving in such a way as to give the impression that subject has a strong ego. This defense mechanism helps subject to feel secure.

NOTES

Person

CLOTHING, COLOR OF

- Any color except white can be used conventionally. It becomes significant only when heavily shaded or used inappropriately.

- When used significantly, it may be interpreted in terms of the general meaning of the color as well as the significance of the part(s) of the body it covers.

CRAYON USED AS PENCIL DRAWING ONLY

- Shallow emotional tone or hostility is indicated.

  See specific color used as pencil drawing (*Person, Black Used as Pencil Drawing*, etc.).

EXPOSED BODY PARTS, COLOR OF

  See specific color used (*Person, Black Used as Pencil Drawing*, etc.).

HAIR

Color of

- The usual colors used for hair on the Person's head are black, brown, red, and yellow. These colors would not be significant unless heavily shaded.

- All other colors so used would be bizarre and therefore pathological unless satisfactorily explained. Once it is determined that the use of the color is significant, the clinician might try applying the general significance of the color to the subject's fantasy activity or attitude towards intellectual activity.

Heavily shaded with black

- Anxiety and/or depression concerning intellect and/or fantasies.

NOTES

HAIR (continued)

Heavily shaded with red
- Subject may engage in fantasies of an erotic nature.

Heavily shaded with yellow
- Very likely engages in hostile fantasies, but may be expressing hostility towards intellectual activity (e.g., school).

PERSON

Black used as pencil drawing
- Depression and/or anxiety concerning relations with people or person symbolized by drawing.

Blue used as pencil drawing
- Depression of mood tone because of unsatisfactory interpersonal relationships. May apply only to person symbolized by drawing.
- Felt need for control in social interaction.

Blue-green used as pencil drawing
- Subject feels maintaining control is important to feeling of security. May apply only to relationship with person symbolized by drawing.

Brown used as pencil drawing
- Conventional for black subjects.
- When used by white subjects, immature handling of affect is indicated.

Green used as pencil drawing
- Great need to feel secure in interpersonal relationships, thus implying a basic feeling of insecurity in social situations or in relationship with the person symbolized by drawing.

NOTES

PERSON (continued)

Orange used as pencil drawing

- Ambivalent attitudes toward people or person symbolized by drawing.

Purple used as pencil drawing

- Need for power over people or person symbolized by drawing.

Red used as pencil drawing

- Much need for affection from people or person symbolized by drawing.

Red-orange used as pencil drawing

- Ambivalent attitudes toward people or person symbolized by drawing but with a valence towards love, hence a more positive feeling than would be indicated by either orange or yellow-orange.

Rose-pink used as pencil drawing

- Conventional use of color, but when no shading or other colors are used, indicates either a shallow emotional tone or hostility.

White used as pencil drawing

- Strong oppositional tendencies toward people and/or person symbolized by drawing.

- Antisocial attitudes.

- These interpretations apply even when the subject uses the white crayon as an initial guide and then uses a more appropriate color over it. This may be the subject's way of trying to repress or conceal his or her attitudes.

Yellow used as pencil drawing

- Hostility towards people or person symbolized by drawing.

NOTES

PERSON (continued)

Yellow-orange used as pencil drawing

- Ambivalent attitudes toward people or person symbolized by drawing with valence towards hostility.

POCKETS PLACED AT BREASTS, HEAVILY SHADED WITH BLACK

- Depression and/or anxiety concerning oral and affectional deprivation.

NOTES

REFERENCES

Buck, J.N. The H-T-P technique, a qualitative and quantitative scoring manual. *Journal of Clinical Psychology*, 1948, *4*, 317-396.

Buck, J.N. *Administration and interpretation of the H-T-P test: Proceedings of the H-T-P workshop held at Veterans Administration Hospital, Richmond, Virginia, March 31-April 2, 1950.* Los Angeles: Western Psychological Services, 1950.

Buck, J.N. *The House-Tree-Person Technique revised manual.* Los Angeles: Western Psychological Services, 1970.

Hammer, E.F. *The clinical application of projective drawings.* Springfield, IL: Charles C. Thomas, 1958.

Jolles, I. *Children's revision House-Tree-Person (H-T-P) Post-Drawing Interrogation folder.* Los Angeles: Western Psychological Services, 1956.

Machover, K. *Personality projection in the drawing of the human figure.* Springfield, IL: Charles C. Thomas, 1949.